THE
Mitzvah Project
BOOK

Pick & Plan Your Mitzvah Project

Workshop Leader's Guide

The workshop leader's companion to
The Mitzvah Project Book: Making Mitzvah Part of Your Bar/Bat Mitzvah … and Your Life by Liz Suneby and Diane Heiman (published by Jewish Lights).

Liz Suneby and Diane Heiman

Other Bar/Bat Mitzvah Resources from Jewish Lights

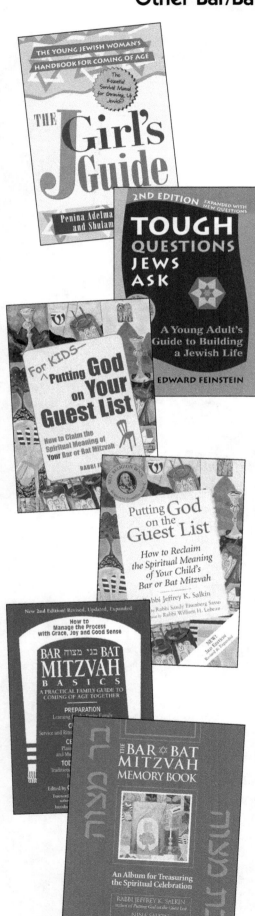

The JGirl's Guide
The Young Jewish Woman's Handbook for Coming of Age
By Penina Adelman, Ali Feldman and Shulamit Reinharz
What does it mean to become a Jewish woman? A first-of-its-kind book of practical, real-world advice using Judaism as a compass for the journey through adolescence. A fun survival guide for girls ages 11 and up.
6 x 9, 240 pp, Quality PB Original, 978-1-58023-215-9

Also Available: *The JGirl's Teacher's and Parent's Guide*
By Miriam P. Polis with Shulamit Reinharz
8½ x 11, 56 pp, PB, 978-1-58023-225-8

Tough Questions Jews Ask, 2nd Ed.
A Young Adult's Guide to Building a Jewish Life
By Rabbi Edward Feinstein
What your rabbi probably never told you—about God, belief, the meaning of life and more—but could have, if you had only asked. New edition, expanded with three new questions! For ages 11 and up.
6 x 9, 160 pp, Quality PB Original, 978-1-58023-454-2

Also Available: *Tough Questions Jews Ask Teacher's Guide*
8½ x 11, 72 pp, PB, 978-1-58023-187-9

For Kids—Putting God on Your Guest List, 2nd Ed.
How to Claim the Spiritual Meaning of Your Bar or Bat Mitzvah
By Rabbi Jeffrey K. Salkin
An important resource to help kids ages 11 to 13 spiritually prepare for their bar/bat mitzvah.
6 x 9, 144 pp, Quality PB Original, 978-1-58023-187-9

Putting God on the Guest List, 3rd Ed.
How to Reclaim the Spiritual Meaning of Your Child's Bar or Bat Mitzvah
By Rabbi Jeffrey K. Salkin
Foreword by Rabbi Sandy Eisenberg Sasso
Today's most influential book about finding core spiritual values.
6 x 9, 224 pp, Quality PB, 978-1-58023-222-7
Hardcover, 978-1-58023-260-9

Also available: *Putting God on the Guest List Teacher's Guide*
8½ x 11, 48 pp, PB, 978-1-58023-226-5

Bar/Bat Mitzvah Basics, 2nd Ed.
A Practical Family Guide to Coming of Age Together
Edited by Cantor Helen Leneman
Foreword by Rabbi Jeffrey K. Salkin, author of *Putting God on the Guest List*
Introduction by Rabbi Julie Gordon
How to manage the process with grace, joy and good sense.
6 x 9, 240 pp, Quality PB Original, 978-1-58023-151-0

The Bar/Bat Mitzvah Memory Book, 2nd Ed.
An Album for Treasuring the Spiritual Celebration
By Rabbi Jeffrey K. Salkin and Nina Salkin
A unique album for preserving the spiritual memories of the day, and for recording plans for the Jewish future ahead.
8 x 10, 48 pp, 2-color text, Deluxe Hardcover w/ ribbon marker, 978-1-58023-263-0

THE
Mitzvah
Project
BOOK

Pick & Plan
Your Mitzvah Project

Workshop Leader's Guide

The workshop leader's companion to
*The Mitzvah Project Book: Making Mitzvah Part of Your
Bar/Bat Mitzvah ... and Your Life* by Liz Suneby and Diane Heiman
(published by Jewish Lights).

Liz Suneby and Diane Heiman

For People of All Faiths, All Backgrounds
JEWISH LIGHTS Publishing

The Mitzvah Project Book: Pick & Plan Your Mitzvah Project Workshop Leader's Guide

2012 Paperback Edition, First Printing
© 2012 by Liz Suneby and Diane Heiman

Manufactured in the United States of America

Cover and Interior Design: Heather Pelham
Cover Art: Laurel Molk

For People of All Faiths, All Backgrounds
Published by Jewish Lights Publishing
www.jewishlights.com

Contents

Introduction

Through fun activities, the "Pick & Plan Your Mitzvah Project Workshop" helps kids come up with meaningful project ideas that fit their interests, talents, and time commitments … and builds excitement for them to get started.

Whether your workshop participants are interested in mitzvah projects for their Bar/Bat Mitzvah, Mitzvah Day, or any *tikkun olam* (repairing the world) initiative, you can select and modify the activities in this guide to fit their needs. Or, perhaps these activities will inspire creative ideas of your own.

Who Should Attend

Preteen and teen kids with or without parents.

Workshop Goals

For each participant to:

- leave with at least one idea for a mitzvah project he or she is excited about
- see the connection between interests, talents, and the ability to make the world a better place
- dispel mitzvah myths
  - I am one person; I can't make a difference
  - I have no time for a mitzvah project
- understand that mitzvah is not a one-time wonder, but a lifelong commitment to *tikkun olam*

The authors are available to lead workshops and to answer questions.
Please contact them at mitzvahprojectbook@gmail.com.

Activities

Select the activities that you feel are the best fit for your objectives, available time, and age range of participants.

Workshop Opener

Introduce yourself and ask participants to introduce themselves. Depending on available time and the size of the group, you could ask participants to only share their name, or add something about themselves and what they hope to get out of the workshop.

Welcome the group and share your goals for the workshop (please refer to "Workshop Goals" in the Introduction).

Thinking about the Changes
You Want to See in the World

Time: 10–15 minutes

Materials: None needed

Goal: Get kids to brainstorm the issues that matter most to them.

 Getting Started

Ask participants:

- "What is the first thing you would fix in the world?"
- "Which issue do you think everyone should care about?"
- "Is there something you wish would no longer be a school, community, or world problem?"

What's a Mitzvah?

Time: 5–15 minutes

Materials: Flip chart/white board and markers

Goal: Get kids thinking about the importance of taking personal
            responsibility for repairing the world.

✓ Getting Started

Ask participants: "What does *mitzvah* mean to you?" (Either go around the room and ask each person for a definition or let people volunteer to offer a definition.) Write down all of the ideas for the group to see.

Share the literal translation of *mitzvah,* "commandment of the Jewish law," and the common usage, "good deed." Compare/contrast how these meanings relate to the group's ideas.

Display both or either of these well-known rabbinic sayings from the Talmud for all to see:

> "If I am not for myself, who will be for me? But if I am only for myself, what am I? And if not now, when?"
>
> (AVOT 1:14)

> "You are not obligated to complete the work, but neither are you free to desist from it."
>
> (AVOT 2:21)

Addressing each quote, ask participants: "What do you think this quote means and how does it relate to the concept of taking personal responsibility for mitzvot?"

The Mitzvah Apprentice

Time: 30–40 minutes

Materials: Paper, pencils, flip chart/white board, markers, and copies of
            The Mitzvah Project Book

Goal: Encourage healthy competition to generate creative yet doable
            mitzvah project ideas.

✓ Explain the Activity

"Have you ever watched *The Apprentice*? You are about to become *Mitzvah Apprentice* contestants. I am going to break you into groups and give each group a mitzvah project challenge. You will be given a mitzvah *type* and *topic*. You will then come up with an idea for a project and present the idea to the other groups in 3 minutes or less. One person in your group will be the Chief Executive Officer (or CEO), who will write down the group's idea and present it to us."

✓ Getting Started

Ask the group to brainstorm *types* of mitzvot: "What are different ways to perform mitzvot?"

Write down the answers for all to see. Prompt: "You could raise money, collect items to donate, volunteer your time and skills, or be an advocate (make the public and/or elected officials aware of an issue through presentations and writing)."

Break participants into four groups, or however many mitzvah types participants have brainstormed. If adults are participating, assign an adult to each group. Give each group a sheet of paper, pencils, and a copy of *The Mitzvah Project Book.*

Assign the CEO role. You could select the person whose birthday is closest to the date of the workshop, the oldest person in the group, etc. Assign each group one of the mitzvah types: raise money, collect items to donate, volunteer your time and skills, be an advocate, etc. Assign *all* groups one of the mitzvah topics from *The Mitzvah Project Book* so that all groups are working with the same topic:

Arts & Crafts	Health
Clothes & Fashion	Music & Dance
Computers & Technology	Sports
Food & Cooking	Environment
Movies & Drama	Family
Reading & Writing	Friends, Neighbors & Your Community
Animals	Global Community
Camp	Israel
Fitness	Jewish Heritage

(You can assign one or have participants vote and let majority rule.)

Explain parameters: "To complete your mitzvah project, assume that adults will provide transportation if necessary. You can use items from home, and you can spend up to $50.00 for supplies, if needed."

Give the groups 10–15 minutes to brainstorm ideas and pick the idea they want to present. Give the groups 10–15 minutes to complete the "Mitzvah Project Planning Guide" on pp. xviii–xix to present their idea. Give the groups 3 minutes each to present their ideas.

It is up to the workshop leader to decide if he/she wants to have judges and a winning team, but it is not necessary to do so.

To wrap up, emphasize how each group offered a unique approach, demonstrating that there are many, many ways to help others.

The Mitzvah Circle

Time: 15–30 minutes

Materials: 3 x 5 index cards and pencils

Goal: Generate mitzvah project ideas relevant to each participant's stated interest or talent.

✔ Explain the Activity

"We are all going to help each other come up with mitzvah project ideas that relate to the things we love to do. Everyone in the room will write down *one* interest or talent on the front of an index card. It could be a school subject (such as science), an after-school/extracurricular activity (such as playing tennis or piano), a hobby (such as origami), or an everyday activity (such as cooking, listening to music, or reading)."

"Then, you'll pass the card around the circle, and each person will write down one mitzvah project idea relating to whatever you wrote on the front. We'll keep passing the card around until everyone has added an idea, and when your card gets back to you, you will have lots of ideas for how to use your interest/talent to help others."

"For example, if 'poetry' is on the front of the card, here are some possible mitzvah project ideas you could suggest:

- Create get-well cards with poems inside and give the cards to a children's hospital to distribute to patients.
- Write a poem about an issue you care about, like recycling, and submit it to your school and town newspapers.
- Read and write poetry with kids in a homeless shelter, day care center, or after-school program for underprivileged children.
- Read poetry to elders at a retirement community.
- Buy poetry books you love with money you earn or receive as gifts and donate them to a library that is in need of books."

✔ Getting Started

Seat participants in circles of eight maximum. Give each participant an index card and pencil.

"Write your name and *one* thing you love on the front/unlined side of the index card. Pass the card to the right."

"Write one mitzvah project idea that relates to the interest on the lined side of the card. Hold the card until everyone is finished. I will let you know when to pass it."

When everyone is finished: "Flip the card over to the front and pass to the right again." Prompt people NOT to read what others have suggested until they have thought of their own idea. (It stifles the imagination.)

8

Repeat these instructions until each participant has their own card back.

Ask for volunteers to share their interest and the mitzvah project suggestions generated by the activity.

Ready, Set, Mitzvah:
Follow-On Activity to the Mitzvah Circle

Time: ~10 minutes

Materials: Copies of *The Mitzvah Project Book* and pencils

Goal: See how to turn ideas into action plans.

✓ Explain the Activity

"Now it is time to turn your favorite idea into the start of an action plan. Pull out your card and pick your favorite idea."

✓ Getting Started

Hand out copies of *The Mitzvah Project Book* to each participant and ask them to turn to "The Mitzvah Project Planning Guide" (pp. xxviii–xix).

"Using that one idea, start filling out the 'Mitzvah Project Planning Guide.'" You can walk participants through the areas of the guide before they start.

Assure participants that they will not be able to complete the guide, but they can start making a plan. If parents are present, they can be very helpful here.

Liz Suneby and Diane Heiman are co-authors of *The Mitzvah Project Book: Making Mitzvah Part of Your Bar/Bat Mitzvah … and Your Life, It's a … It's a … It's a Mitzvah* (ages 3–6) and the Children's Choice Award winner *See What You Can Be: Explore Careers That Could Be for You!*

Praise for *The Mitzvah Project Book: Making Mitzvah Part of Your Bar/Bat Mitzvah … and Your Life*

"A treasure-trove of amazing ideas…. Perfect for any B'nai Mitzvah-to-be, and also fantastic for any older children, tweens and teenagers who want to find a way to have a meaningful impact in their local or global community."
—**Rabbi Danya Ruttenberg**, author, *Surprised By God: How I Learned to Stop Worrying and Love Religion*

"Full of fun, engaging and valuable activities! Authors Diane Heiman and Liz Suneby do a great service to the Jewish people and our world, making today's mitzvah projects even more accessible and meaningful for B'nai Mitzvah and beyond."
—**Rabbi Joel Sisenwine**, Temple Beth Elohim, Wellesley, Massachusetts; rabbinic chair, Union for Reform Judaism's Joint Commission on Worship, Music and Religious Living

"A must-read for every Bar/Bat Mitzvah student, parents, rabbis and educators…. Brilliantly reminds us that there is no better way to enter Jewish adulthood than to begin to put a vision for a more just and holy world into action."
—**Rabbi Shmuly Yanklowitz**, founder/president, Uri L'Tzedek, The Orthodox Social Justice Movement

"Helps make the process of becoming a Bar/Bat Mitzvah relevant and meaningful. A great addition to this important life cycle!"
—**Rabbi Jamie Korngold**, The Adventure Rabbi; author, *The God Upgrade: Finding Your 21st-Century Spirituality in Judaism's 5,000-Year-Old Tradition*

"Speaks to our children simply and naturally, fanning the flames of their passions and interests and offering creative ideas so that the performance of mitzvot can be woven into their daily lives."
—**Cantor Jodi Sufrin**, Temple Beth Elohim, Wellesley, Massachusetts

"A wonderful source guide for a new generation of Jewish children and their parents."
—**Cantor Mikhail Manevich**, Washington Hebrew Congregation, Washington, DC

Bar/Bat Mitzvah Gift Books from Jewish Lights

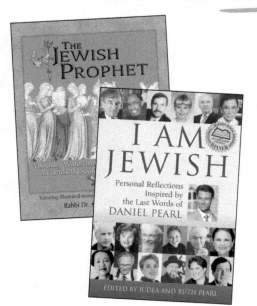

The Jewish Prophet
Visionary Words from Moses and Miriam to Henrietta Szold and A. J. Heschel
By Rabbi Dr. Michael J. Shire
Featuring illustrated manuscripts from the British Library.
6½ x 8½, 128 pp, 123 full-color illus., Hardcover, 978-1-58023-168-8

I Am Jewish
Personal Reflections Inspired by the Last Words of Daniel Pearl
Edited by Judea and Ruth Pearl
6 x 9, 304 pp, Deluxe PB w/ flaps, 978-1-58023-259-3

Also Available: *I Am Jewish Teacher's Guide*
8½ x 11, 10 pp, PB, 978-1-58023-219-7

For People of All Faiths, All Backgrounds
JEWISH LIGHTS Publishing

www.jewishlights.com

 Find us on Facebook®
Facebook is a registered trademark of Facebook, Inc.

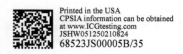